W9-ASY-383

The Siamang Gibbons
An Ape Family

The Siamang Gibbons

An Ape Family

ALICE SCHICK

Pictures by Joel Schick

WESTWIND PRESS

LIBRARY OF CONGRESS NUMBER: 75-38550

Printed in the United States of America.

Published by   Westwind Press, A Division of
                Raintree Publishers Limited
                Milwaukee, Wisconsin 53203

Distributed to the trade by
                Follett Publishing Company
                1010 West Washington Street
                Chicago, Illinois 60607
Library Edition L-0639
Trade Edition T-0639

LIBRARY OF CONGRESS CATALOGING IN PUBLICATION DATA

Schick, Alice.
  The siamang gibbons.

  SUMMARY: Traces a family of gibbons from the Sumatran
jungle to the Milwaukee County Zoo.
  1. Siamang—Juvenile literature. (1. Siamang.
2. Gibbons) 1. Schick, Joel. 11. Title.
QL737.P96S35   599'.882   75-38550
ISBN 0-8172-0506-3
ISBN 0-8172-0507-1 lib. bdg.

For Grundoon

Acknowledgments

This story of a family of siamang gibbons could not have been written without the cooperation of the marvelous staff of the Milwaukee County Zoo. George Speidel, the Zoo Director, encouraged the project from the beginning and took time out from a demanding schedule to review the manuscript and write an introduction for the book. Leonard Wehr, Sam La Malfa, and Bill Groth contributed much to the spirit of the book by sharing with me their understanding and affection for the zoo animals, particularly the siamangs.

Greysolynne Fox is not on the Milwaukee Zoo staff, but was nevertheless instrumental in the creation of this book. She has spent hundreds of hours observing the Milwaukee siamangs and probably knows the animals better than anyone else. Greysolynne generously shared all her information (which would have been unavailable elsewhere) with me, not only sending me copies of papers she had written, but also answering specific questions at length. Finally, she reviewed the manuscript with great care, helping to assure its scientific accuracy.

Alice Schick

November, 1975

Contents

Foreword

With *The Siamang Gibbons*: *An Ape Family*, Alice Schick has written a book that is as interesting as it is educational, a combination that makes for excellent reading. Ms. Schick is a very good storyteller, and adults as well as children will enjoy this book.

In the beginning she describes the Sumatran jungle—the tree-dimmed first floor, where tigers and elephants roam in lush semi-darkness, and the canopy, where the energetic siamang gibbons swing through the trees with the greatest of ease.

This book is about a siamang family, and readers should find their lives as interesting as a peek through the window of the house next door. The head of this ape household, Unk, was born in the jungle but finally established his family at the Milwaukee County Zoo.

Unk's story is a success story. Once a sickly weakling, he developed into a powerful fighter and a doting father. Unk's story also is a love story, filled with suspense. Will Unk's intended bride, Suzy, survive the courtship? Will the two apes live happily ever after?

In addition to accurately and sympathetically describing one of the world's most exciting animals—the siamang—Ms. Schick also applies the same accuracy and understanding in telling of the Milwaukee County Zoo's concern for the world's animals. Our animals are happy and healthy, and we have had a number of successful breeding programs, including that of the siamang.

We are pleased that the public appreciates our efforts and continues to visit the zoo in increasingly large numbers. In 1974, more than a million and a half people visited the zoo. In the years to come, we expect many more to visit our animals. And I'm sure that some of the most popular animals will continue to be the siamangs, whose lives Ms. Schick has portrayed with such skill and devotion.

George Speidel
DIRECTOR
THE MILWAUKEE COUNTY ZOO

The Siamang Gibbons
An Ape Family

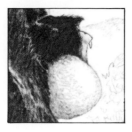

CHAPTER ONE

Sumatra

Dawn in the jungle. On the forest floor the heavy blackness of the night was replaced by the soft greenish light of day. The bright tropical sun was hidden by the dense canopy of vegetation. Only on the streams and the rocky mountain tops where no trees grew was the sky visible. Everywhere else the light at ground level was dim and cool.

A dark striped tiger returned to its den, lay down and began licking a front paw. During the night the tiger had hunted successfully, surprising a sleeping wild hog. Now it

3

would doze, perhaps waking during the day for a drink and a swim in the stream. But for the most part it was a night creature, and the jungle now belonged to the creatures of the day.

At the edge of the stream butterflies appeared by the thousands. Pheasants awakened and patrolled the forest floor, scratching about for insects and seeds. Elephants began to feed, browsing on the trees and bushes for the many pounds of vegetation each animal needed every day. All the other large herbivores of the jungle—the wild hogs, the deer, the tapirs, and the rhinos—also were animals of the daylight. They too awakened and began the essential business of finding food.

Thirty feet above the ground, in the jungle's middle layer, the night shift also gave way to the day. A slow loris blinked its large round eyes and began to settle itself into a comfortable position for sleeping. Unlike most primates, the loris was a nocturnal creature, and even the dim daylight of the jungle bothered the animal's eyes. A clouded leopard, a small cat with beautiful markings, had spent the night prowling the trees and bushes of the middle layer in search of sleeping birds and rodents. With the approach of day, this predator returned to ground level to sleep.

The biggest change in the middle layer at dawn was an increase in noise. The night animals were generally quiet, either predators trying to sneak up on unwary prey, or small and defenseless creatures trying to avoid notice. Now, at dawn, the nervous, silent mice were replaced by the larger, exuberant squirrels. The squirrels chattered and bickered incessantly, and chased one another wildly through the trees, with much noisy shaking of branches. And with the coming of daylight, bird song began. Birds of a hundred different species awakened and opened their beaks to attract mates or announce their ownership of nesting territories.

Above the middle layer, day began too in the top level of the forest. The jungle canopy, formed by the interlocking branches and leaves of trees more than one hundred feet tall, was the reason for the dimness of the light on the forest floor. And the dense vegetation of the topmost jungle layer provided homes for many animals active by day.

Naturally, some species of birds preferred the canopy to the middle layer of the jungle. But there were reptiles too, climbing lizards that lived their whole lives in the treetops. Even more surprising, the canopy was home to frogs and insects. They lived in miniature, sky-high swamps created by epiphytes, plants that grew on the tall trees but took their nourishment directly from the surrounding jungle air.

But the jungle canopy at dawn really belonged to the primates. At sunup, vast troops of gray leaf monkeys awakened and scampered through the branches. Solitary, slow-moving red orangutans opened their eyes and stretched lazily. Only the young animals seemed eager to vacate their leafy nests. The older, more experienced orangs seemed to know that the jungle held plenty of food even for late sleepers.

Shortly after sunrise, the canopy exploded with sound, as the white-handed gibbons began their morning calls. Every gibbon family in the jungle seemed to be calling at once, a tremendous chorus, like the song of ten million birds. Within thirty minutes the gibbon chorus ended as the animals moved off to their favorite feeding places. The end of their singing did not bring quiet to the canopy, however.

Suddenly, one treetop was alive with great booming, whooping noises. When this calling stopped, similar noises began in a nearby tree. The sounds passed from tree to tree as the siamang families reaffirmed their territorial borders. With the siamangs' calls, the day in the Sumatran jungle had officially begun.

The siamang gibbons and the smaller white-handed gibbons were closely related species. Their habits and food preferences were similar. Yet both species survived in the Sumatran jungle because it was an incredibly rich environment. Each layer of the forest provided abundant food of many varieties. And so the jungle was home to many animals.

Very few humans lived in the jungle. The people preferred to settle at the jungle's edge, building their small villages, called kampongs, in open areas where they could see the sky. Most of the people were farmers, raising goats and a few crops. And most rarely ventured into the jungle. They feared the strange, dim light and the unknown noises. They feared becoming lost where the sky was hidden. They feared tigers and poisonous snakes.

Only one man in the local kampong liked the jungle. Rami, like his neighbors, was a farmer, but he often left his fields for days at a time. Alone, he traveled deep into the jungle to search for wild cinnamon, a product much in demand among traders from the coast.

Rami cleared a tiny patch of jungle land near a stream and built a simple camp. His food came from the forest: fish from the stream, fruit from the trees, and wild herbs from the bushes. Each day he wandered through the hillsides in search of cinnamon. When he had enough to fill the basket strapped to his back, Rami returned to the kampong.

Rami enjoyed the extra income the cinnamon brought. But even more than that, he liked being by himself in the jungle. As he came to know the forest he lost his fears. He moved quietly, almost becoming a part of the jungle. After a time, the secretive animals grew used to him and no longer fled at his approach. He could watch them as they went about their normal activities.

Six siamang gibbon families lived near Rami's jungle camp. Although the families lived close together, each had its own territory, a few acres of jungle canopy. The great calling sessions reminded all the siamangs in the district just which territory belonged to each family.

Rami's camp was included in the territory of one of the siamang families, so he saw more of these animals than any of the others. The siamang family consisted of an enormous male, a female only slightly smaller, and their three children.

The oldest was a seven-year-old female, almost completely grown. The middle child was a male, two years younger and still a playful juvenile. The youngest child, a female, was not yet two years old, still an infant.

Rami never grew tired of watching the siamangs. Their behavior seemed almost human, and he began to see the animals as distinct individuals, even giving them human names. He called the mother Tarag and the father Toba. He did not name the two younger children because their personalities were not yet completely formed, but the oldest child he called Singkil. Singkil was the coastal town where Rami's cinnamon was sold, and the word sounded beautiful to Rami's ears. It seemed fitting to give a beautiful name to his favorite siamang.

At twenty-two pounds, Singkil was almost as large as she would ever be, about average size for a female siamang. Her black fur was exceptionally long and soft-looking. When Singkil moved through an open place, her fur shone in the sunlight. Like all siamangs, she was built for moving through the trees. Her arms were extremely long. Her hands too were elongated, with very long fingers. Her face was black and nearly hairless, with dark, sad-looking eyes.

This morning was Rami's first at his jungle camp in many weeks. He arose before the first light and prepared his breakfast. From his location on the ground, Rami could just make out the forms of the siamangs high overhead. The animals were still asleep. Tarag slept sitting up on the middle of a branch. The youngest member of the family, the little female, slept with her. The baby clung to Tarag's chest, encircling the mother's body with four long, skinny limbs. Tarag wrapped her own arms around the baby, so its head and body were totally protected. On a branch nearby, the five-year-old male lay curled into a tight ball. Toba, the father, slept sprawled along the same branch, with one hand on his sleeping son. Twenty feet away from the rest of the family, Singkil slept alone.

To Rami, Singkil looked like a lonely outcast. And in a way, she was exactly that. At seven, Singkil was almost mature, and like all grown-up siamangs, she would be forced to leave her family. Tarag and Toba were mates for life. They were good parents, but so jealous that they could not tolerate the presence of another adult siamang. Even the fact that Singkil was their own child made no difference. She would soon be driven away, and the strong bond between her parents would be undisturbed.

The sun had been up for more than an hour when the siamangs began to stir. Toba opened his eyes and rolled over onto his back. He looked at his son, as if hoping to find the youngster awake. But, seeing no movement, he shifted position again and closed his eyes. The little female wriggled free of Tarag's embrace and began to swing idly on a vine. Tarag was now awake too, but she seemed unwilling to move just yet. She watched the baby with half-closed eyes.

After a few minutes the young male awakened and sat up. Instantly Toba opened his eyes and tugged on his son's fur. The young animal obediently started to groom his father, carefully picking through Toba's fur, separating the hairs and removing small bits of dirt. This activity was pleasant and relaxing as well as useful for both animals. Grooming one another kept the siamangs clean and reinforced their family ties, too.

Next Singkil began to stir. She noticed her small sister playing on the vine and began to move toward her. Suddenly Tarag was wide awake. Every muscle in her body tensed, and she started to open and close her mouth rapidly, smacking her lips together. She was obviously angry. Singkil recognized the threat and quickly retreated to her sleeping place. Eyeing her mother, she showed her distress by holding her arms out sideways, then shaking her head, hands, and arms repeatedly for nearly a minute.

Neither Tarag nor Toba objected to Singkil's participation in the family calling. The siamangs' morning calls began when, half an hour after waking up, Toba inflated his throat sac. This was a pouch of hairless skin that usually hung in loose folds beneath the animal's chin. Uninflated, the sac lay almost hidden in the siamang's fur. But when Toba breathed in a great gulp of air to inflate it, the throat sac bulged like a giant balloon, looking ready to burst. The throat sac acted as a sound amplifier, enabling siamang calls to be heard for great distances.

Toba began with single deep booming noises. Soon, Tarag joined in with booms of her own. Toba's calling changed to a series of short barks, as if he were giving a "call to attention." Tarag began to make barking noises which rapidly grew louder and faster. Meanwhile, Toba's calls consisted of long screams and barks. When Tarag's barking reached its peak, Toba let out a loud *ya-hoo*. This seemed to be a signal to the three youngsters to join in. With their smaller throat sacs, the young siamangs made clear, bell-like calls.

As the calling continued, the siamangs grew more and more excited. They ran upright along the branches, their hands held high above their heads. They swung on vines, using one, two, three, or four limbs. They moved quickly through the branches in the arm-over-arm motion called brachiation.

No matter how often Rami witnessed the siamangs' calling, he found it exciting and astonishing. He watched and listened for twenty-five minutes, until the calling subsided and was taken up by another siamang family nearby. Then, with the siamangs' song still echoing in his ears, Rami moved off in search of wild cinnamon.

The siamangs soon moved off, too. The family traveled in single file, with Tarag, the mother, in the lead. She brachiated confidently through the canopy, hooking the fingers of one hand onto a branch or vine, while reaching forward with the fingers of the opposite hand to the next holding place. Her super-long fingers and hands gave her a sure grip. Tarag moved rapidly, but not as quickly as she could. She avoided making great flying leaps from one tree to another. Frequently she turned to check on the little female behind her. The baby was just beginning to travel on her own and would require experience and growth before she became an accomplished brachiator.

Behind the youngest member of the family came the five-year-old male, and then came Singkil. Since Tarag was not moving too fast, the two older children had no trouble keeping up. There was even time for a bit of play. They stopped traveling to chase each other through the treetops in a brief but wild game of tag. Tarag was occupied with leading the group and watching the baby so, for once, she didn't interfere with Singkil's activities. Toba, bringing up the rear of the family procession, also left his daughter alone. Singkil made the most of her rare opportunity to play with her brother. Both animals seemed to enjoy the game, although Singkil, the larger of the two, played roughly, totally dominating the younger gibbon.

The siamangs arrived at their destination, a huge fig tree at the edge of their territory. Figs were a favorite food of the gibbons. Unfortunately, the sweet, sticky red figs were a favorite food of other animals as well, and the siamangs found their fig tree occupied.

A large hornbill was easily displaced. As the five siamangs crashed through the foliage, the bird took off, so anxious to avoid the family that it dropped the fig it was holding in its beak. The fruit fell to the ground far below, where it would likely become a special treat for a jungle-floor animal.

A more difficult problem was the orangutans. There were three of the red apes in the fig tree—a big male, and a female with a large infant. The orangs were not a family—unlike gibbons, the orangs were solitary except for mothers with young—but they fed together peacefully in the tree. When the siamang family appeared, the little orangutan moved closer to its mother. The two adults continued to feed. The unexcitable orangs seemed perfectly content to share the fig harvest with the other apes.

The siamangs were far less generous. For several seconds, five dark faces glared at the orangs from a nearby branch. Then Toba leaped into the fig tree, crashing down with all his weight and shaking branches furiously. This was followed by four smaller crashes as the rest of the siamang family joined him.

At once, Singkil and her brother headed toward the baby orang. Perhaps they merely wanted to play, but the mother orangutan saw their behavior as a threat. She gathered up her baby and held it close to her as she watched the black apes warily.

The five siamangs seemed to be having a wonderful time. They swung and ran through the tree, picking fruit, sometimes eating it and sometimes tossing it away. They concentrated their actions in the area where the mother orang sat with her baby. After only a few minutes, the harassed orangutan, too disturbed to eat, gave up and moved off with her baby.

The first battle won, the siamangs turned their attention to the big male orang. The red ape was a magnificent animal, five times Toba's weight, with powerful arms and an imposing facial expression. Nevertheless, the gibbons showed him no respect. Without hesitation, the siamang family began to torment the orangutan. They danced all around him, causing a terrible commotion. They shook branches and shrieked. Finally, Toba plucked a fig and tossed it at the orang, hitting him in the side of the head. The red ape was not hurt by the fruit, but he had had enough. Slowly and deliberately, he brachiated away.

The siamangs now had the fig tree all to themselves, and they settled down to feed. They were picky eaters, selecting only the best fruits, then taking apart the figs with great delicacy and discarding seeds and bad spots. They could afford to be choosy because the jungle always held far more food than they needed. If their favorite figs were too ripe for their taste, the siamangs could eat grapes or plums or mangoes. They liked leaf shoots and stems and flower buds, too. And there were always fat caterpillars, ants, and termites available for occasional snacks.

The siamangs fed together for two hours. Once, Singkil scampered over to a nearby tree, where three large branches came together to form a natural bowl. The bowl was always filled with rainwater—a canopy-level waterhole handy for animals who rarely descended to the ground. Singkil drank in typical gibbon fashion. She dipped a hand into the water, then licked the water off the fur on the back of her knuckles.

She repeated this action several times, until her thirst was quenched.

During the morning feeding session, peace reigned in the siamang family. Singkil was permitted to eat with the others. Later, though, after the gibbons had traveled to a favorite midday resting place, her parents' hostility surfaced again. The two youngest siamangs were playing, chasing each other through the trees in a circular path. Singkil tried to join in by jumping out from behind a clump of leaves to surprise her brother. Tarag rushed at her, forcing her to retreat. Singkil then approached her father, asking to be groomed. Toba bared his teeth at her, then moved away, finally sitting down to be groomed by Tarag. Singkil shook her arms in frustration, then settled back morosely to groom herself. Although she was obviously upset, she was a fastidious groomer, removing all traces of the sticky figs from her lovely fur.

After the midday "siesta," the siamang family began to travel again. During the afternoon, they moved through the trees of their small territory, stopping here and there to feed. The animals stayed close together; even Singkil remained in sight of her parents. They saw no other siamang families, because each group stuck to its own territory. As the day went on, the siamangs spent more and more time grooming each other, and less time feeding.

In late afternoon, the siamangs' travel suddenly seemed purposeful again. As usual, they moved in single file with Tarag leading. Within ten minutes they were back in the area of Rami's camp and had decided on a sleeping tree for the night. They had several favorite trees—they usually didn't choose the same tree two nights in a row, but they usually chose a place they had slept before. An hour of settling down and grooming followed.

By the time Rami returned to his camp, the siamangs were asleep; Tarag with the baby, Toba with the young male, and Singkil alone. As darkness fell, the black forms of the sleeping gibbons melted into the canopy leaves. The siamang day was over. Once again the jungle belonged to the creatures of the night.

CHAPTER TWO

Unk

Six months passed before Rami returned to the jungle. During the time he had harvested his crops from his fields near the kampong, important changes had taken place in the life of the siamang family. Tarag had a new baby. Like all newborn apes, it was weak and helpless. The baby slept most of the time, waking only to nurse or to be groomed. It stayed with Tarag constantly, clinging to her chest hair. Tarag supported the infant atop her bent legs as she brachiated through the canopy.

19

The baby required nearly all of Tarag's attention. The little female had begun to spend more time with Toba, who, like all siamang fathers, played an important role in family life. He gave the older infant the protection and affection she still needed.

The five-year-old male was almost independent. Although not yet full grown, he had mastered the skills needed for life in the treetops. He no longer slept close to Toba—that place had been taken over by his younger sister. Nevertheless, he was still very much a part of the family, feeding peacefully with the others, playing, grooming and being groomed, and sleeping in the communal tree.

Singkil had been driven from the family. Her parents no longer permitted her to sleep, feed, or play with the others. She was not included in calling or grooming sessions. She remained on the edge of her family's territory, as if she hoped to be readmitted to the group.

Rami felt sorry for her. It seemed that an animal who had spent her whole life in the close company of others must feel lonely by herself. One morning, before the siamangs called, Rami watched the young male approach Singkil. She saw her brother and, with obvious pleasure, ran to meet him. The two animals came toward each other quickly, without hesitation, running upright along a branch. Both gibbons wore facial expressions that looked like human smiles. When they met, they threw their arms around one another, hugging like long-lost friends. Squealing with delight, the siamang brother and sister sat down for a mutual grooming session.

Rami never knew it, but he had witnessed the last real contact between Singkil and her family. Shortly afterward, a male siamang about Singkil's age entered the area. He too had recently been pushed out of his family. It was time for him to find a mate of his own, and he soon found Singkil. The young siamangs, eager for companionship, accepted each other almost immediately. During a short and smooth courtship of playing, grooming, and "talking," Singkil and the young male formed a lifelong pair bond.

Finding a mate was simple for a young siamang. Finding a place to live was another matter entirely. Singkil and her mate could not stay near her parents. A siamang family might permit a lone adult to remain at the fringes of their territory, but a new pair of gibbons represented a threat to the established order. If they tried to claim a territory in the immediate area, they would come into conflict with the previous owners.

And of course, like all new siamang pairs, Singkil and her mate did try to establish a territory in the treetops. They did this by calling, announcing their ownership of a section of canopy. Quickly they discovered that every place they claimed already had owners who were not at all reluctant to defend it. Their calling invariably brought attack.

The adult male owner would rush at them fiercely, baring his teeth and screaming. Sometimes the rest of his family would follow, screaming and throwing branches. If the young invaders did not retreat, they risked a nasty bite from the large sharp teeth of a male siamang.

With six families in residence, the area of the rain forest near Rami's camp was filled to capacity with siamang gibbons. Singkil and her mate would have to leave the region if ever they were to find a home of their own. Finally the young siamangs did leave, moving north toward the Ranun River, far from Rami's camp. No human could follow their treetop trail, and Rami did not know where the siamangs had gone. He expected never to see Singkil again.

More than a year later, Rami was hired as a jungle guide by Dieter and Gretchen Hoffmann. The Hoffmanns were animal collectors. They traveled all over the world to capture wild creatures for sale to zoos. The year was 1952, and animal collecting was a perfectly respectable occupation. The wild places of the world seemed vast and indestructible. Animal populations seemed limitless. Surely the capture of small numbers of animals made no difference to a whole species. Few people could foresee the terrible problems of the future—human overpopulation and the destruction of wild habitats. In 1952, many of the best zoos in the world obtained most of their animals from dealers like the Hoffmanns.

Dieter and Gretchen were making their first trip to Sumatra. They hoped to bring back a variety of the island's incredible wildlife, but they were especially interested in animals that were rarely seen in European or American zoos, animals like siamang gibbons. Rami was willing to help the Hoffmanns locate animals. However, he had no intention of taking them to his camp. He did not want any of the siamangs he knew to be captured and sent to zoos thousands of miles away.

Instead they headed north, toward the salt caves. Near the Ranun River were cliffs made of soft, salty white stone. Like most animals, the forest elephants craved salt, and they had the built-in means to get it. Bull elephants stabbed at the soft rock with their tusks, gouging caves out of the cliffs. Cow elephants had no tusks, but helped to enlarge the caves with their feet and trunks and even with their tongues, by licking the salty rock until it crumbled. Countless generations of elephants had used the area, and over the centuries had made some surprisingly large caves, as much as fifteen feet high and thirty feet deep.

Rami knew that the salt caves were congregating places for many different kinds of animals. Perhaps the Hoffmanns could capture some of the wild creatures that visited the elephant caves to eat salt.

When they neared the area of the caves, Gretchen and Dieter instructed their helpers to set up camp nearby. Then they asked Rami to show them the caves. It was late afternoon, and they didn't expect to see much activity before dark. Still, they were anxious to look over the site and develop some work plans. The three humans carried no equipment and moved quickly on the soft forest floor. When they reached their destination they hid behind a clump of bushes. From there they could see the caves without being noticed by any animals who came to lick salt.

From their hiding place, Rami, Dieter, and Gretchen had a clear view of the entrance to a large cave. The cave was too deep, and its ceiling too covered with branches and vines for them to see inside. At the cave opening stood a female muntjac, a small deer with a reddish coat. The doe was licking the base of the cave wall, intent on obtaining salt, apparently unaware of the humans close by. The forest was quiet, and the muntjac seemed to be the only wildlife around.

After a few minutes the doe raised her head and sniffed the air. Suddenly she seemed to sense danger. She gave her warning cry, a series of loud noises like a dog's bark, noises that explain the muntjac's other name—barking deer. The doe turned and bolted into the forest.

An instant later the three humans heard scrambling noises from inside the cave. Before they had time to guess what it was, two hairy black forms emerged. Siamangs! Alarmed by the barking deer, the gibbons were in a terrible hurry. The first siamang did not even stop, but leaped from the top of the cave entrance upward across an open space to a tall tree, and disappeared noisily into the foliage. The second animal hesitated for a moment at the cave entrance. Then it too made a great flying leap, reaching out for the same tree branch.

The second siamang missed. The animal fell forty feet

to the ground. The watching humans held their breath, stunned, waiting for the gibbon to recover. But the siamang lay still.

Rami and the Hoffmanns left their hiding place to investigate. Even as they approached, the siamang did not move. The animal lay on its side. A tiny baby, not more than two months old, still clung to the larger gibbon's fur. This explained why the siamang had fallen. Burdened with the baby, the frightened mother had been unable to leap as well as her mate.

Rami bent down to get a better look. Gently he rolled the animal onto her back. Hoping for signs of life he stared at her face, feeling somehow that he had seen this gibbon before. Suddenly he knew. The lifeless siamang at his feet was Singkil.

Singkil was dead. But miraculously, her baby had survived the fall. Pressed against Singkil's body, clutching her fur with tiny hands, the baby made whimpering noises. Gretchen knelt and carefully detached the little siamang from its mother. At once the baby clasped Gretchen's shirt, clinging as tightly to her as it had to its gibbon mother.

Back in camp the Hoffmanns examined the small creature they had reluctantly adopted. The baby siamang was a male, and very young, probably around five or six weeks old. Like most infant primates, his head looked very large in proportion to his body. His dark eyes, set in a tiny, wrinkled black face, looked enormous. It was hard to escape the feeling that

the baby siamang looked like a little old man. Dieter and Gretchen named him Unk.

In spite of Unk's young age, the Hoffmanns felt reasonably certain he would survive. He had not been injured in the fall that killed his mother, and he appeared to be well-nourished and in good health. Dieter and Gretchen had once cared for an orphaned baby white-handed gibbon, and had devised a nutritious milk formula and later a diet of fruit and grain for it. The same foods would probably be right for a siamang.

If the Hoffmanns were sure they could meet Unk's physical needs, they were far less confident that they could meet his psychological needs. A baby gibbon, they knew, needed affectionate attention from his parents. Living in a family group, watching his parents, a baby learned how to be a gibbon—not only what foods were good to eat and how to move through the treetops, but how to interact with other gibbons. What would happen to a gibbon raised by humans?

The white-handed gibbon the Hoffmanns had raised never learned that she was a gibbon. With human parents, she naturally behaved as if she were human, too. When she grew up, Gretchen and Dieter sent her to live in a zoo, where she had a chance to live with other gibbons. But she was afraid of other gibbons, and even after three years at the zoo, responded affectionately only to humans. Undoubtedly she would never take a gibbon mate.

Dieter and Gretchen worried that the same thing would

happen to Unk. Yet there was nothing they could do to prevent it. Few zoos even had one siamang. And none had a
mated pair who might be able to adopt a siamang orphan.
The Hoffmanns would simply have to do what they could
for Unk and hope for the best.

The baby siamang thrived in the Hoffmanns' care while
they remained in the Sumatran jungle. Trouble did not
arise until Unk was four months old and they returned home
to Germany with a shipment of animals. At first, the trouble
was nothing more than the Hoffmanns' vague feeling that
the little siamang was unhappy. Unk didn't seem to enjoy
his food as much as he once had, and he was eating less. He
played less too, preferring to spend his time clinging to
Gretchen. Finally, although he was kept warm and not
taken outdoors in the chilly European winter, Unk caught
cold and developed pneumonia.

Unk was a very sick little ape. Both a veterinarian and a
pediatrician, who usually treated only human children, were
called in. The two doctors prescribed medicine, but agreed
that the case looked hopeless. Such a delicate young animal,
so far from home and his own kind, would surely die.

The Hoffmanns refused to give up. For six long and
terrible weeks they stayed with Unk around the clock, sleeping in shifts. Their patient needed medicine every two hours,
food to maintain his strength, warmth, and above all, love.
The treatment worked. To the surprise of nearly everyone,
especially the two doctors, and much to the relief of the
Hoffmanns, Unk recovered completely.

Healthy once again, Unk behaved like a totally different ape. He was ten months old, and he quickly made up for lost growing time by developing a huge appetite. Not only did he finish his own meals in record time, he also helped Gretchen and Dieter finish theirs. He became an accomplished thief, sneaking up on the humans at the table, snatching a potato or a handful of string beans from a plate, and swinging away to a high shelf where no one could reach him. The Hoffmanns didn't really mind, but their friends did. They soon found that no one would have supper at their house any more.

Unk loved to play. The Hoffmanns' small house became a substitute jungle, and their furniture soon showed the effects of the siamang's running, jumping, swinging, tearing, and biting. It seemed that he never became tired and he hardly ever slept. Unk sat still only for grooming sessions, which he loved. He offered his long arms to Gretchen or Dieter for grooming, and in return, insisted on grooming his foster parents. He seemed confused by the lack of hair on their arms, but seemed to regard their abundant head hair as a special consolation prize. Eeach day he spent twenty minutes or more grooming Gretchen's hair, using his fingers gently but deftly, and making soft murmuring noises of contentment all the while.

The Hoffmanns knew they would not be able to keep Unk forever. He was rapidly becoming too big and too strong to live free in their house. He was beginning to regard the house as the territory of his family, and beginning to

defend it in normal siamang fashion. When anyone other than Gretchen or Dieter entered, he inflated his throat sac and gave loud calls of alarm. Not surprisingly, most visitors *were* alarmed, and so were the neighbors. And if an intruder was not scared away by the noise, Unk attacked with his teeth.

Reluctantly, the Hoffmanns sold their young siamang to another animal dealer. This man was putting together a shipment of animals to send to the United States. Representatives from several different American zoos would look over the animals, buying those they wanted for their collections. Unk became one small part of that shipment.

Unk was little more than one year old. In the forests of Sumatra, a siamang of that age would live with its parents, almost constantly in contact with them, never out of their sight for more than a few minutes. A wild one-year-old siamang needed its parents. Unk needed his parents, too. And for him, parents meant Dieter and Gretchen. Truly alone for the first time, Unk acted frightened and withdrawn on the trip to the United States. He bit any attendant who tried to comfort him.

By the time the ship docked in New York, Unk looked like anything but a healthy animal. His fur was dull and lifeless, his eyes had lost their sparkle, and he was far too thin. He had developed what looked like a permanent case of the sniffles.

Then there was the problem of his disposition—he behaved aggressively toward everyone. If he was difficult to
handle now, what would he be like in a couple of years,
when his weight doubled and he had an adult set of teeth?
That is, what would he be like if he survived?

Siamang gibbons were zoo rarities, but the animal dealer
could not find anyone who wanted Unk. To all the American
zoo representatives who saw him, this siamang looked like
a bad risk. So Unk was returned to Germany.

The German zoos didn't want him either, but finally the
Hanover Zoo agreed to take him. There, under a program
of intensive medical treatment and good nutrition, Unk
slowly got well again. He was placed in a large, airy cage,
with plenty of room for exercise. Unfortunately, the zoo
could do nothing about his need for companionship.
Gretchen and Dieter visited him once in a while, but they
could neither stay nor take him home with them. There were
no other siamangs in the zoo. And Unk was too big and
aggressive to be placed with any of the smaller gibbons.

Over the next few years, Unk grew into a magnificent
animal. He had long, lustrous black fur, weighed close to
fifty pounds, and was extremely strong. He often hung from
his cage bars by his hands, staring at the zoo visitors. He was
a popular attraction, especially on those occasions when he
inflated his throat sac and let out a whoop or two. But one
sad fact remained: Unk was alone.

CHAPTER THREE

Suzy

Across the Atlantic Ocean, far from the Hanover Zoo, an American zoo official was making plans. George Speidel was the director of the zoo in Milwaukee, Wisconsin. Like many city zoos in the United States and Europe, the Milwaukee Zoo had been constructed in the early years of the twentieth century. At that time, the goal of most zoos was to display as many different kinds of animals as possible. Cages often were small to save space, and quite bare to make them easy to clean. Usually, there was room for only one of each kind of

33

animal. Breeding wild animals in captivity did not seem very important. Most zoo officials at the turn of the century considered it easier and cheaper to replace animals that died with newly captured ones from the wild.

Fifty years later, some zoo directors felt differently. The traditional way of running a zoo seemed wrong to them. The public could learn very little about animal behavior by watching an animal alone in a tiny, barred cement cage. Zoo animals often seemed unhappy, and many died at very young ages. And it seemed dishonest for zoo officials to promote conservation of animals in the wild while they continued to capture large numbers of wild animals for zoo displays.

Zoos would be better places for both people and animals, these zoo officials decided, if each zoo were to display fewer different kinds of animals but more individuals of each kind. Each pair or group of animals could be given enough space and the proper conditions to enable them to behave much as they would in the wild. Such an arrangement would encourage breeding, thereby reducing the need for zoos to capture animals from their natural habitats. It would also make zoo-going a more valuable educational experience for the public.

The only problem was money. It would be terribly expensive to modernize a fifty-year-old zoo, to turn tiny, dark cages into large, airy enclosures. Many of the old city zoos might have to be rebuilt from the ground up. That would cost a fortune, literally millions of dollars. Most zoo directors knew they could not raise so much money. If they wanted to improve conditions, they would have to proceed very slowly, one small step at a time.

George Speidel was fortunate. When Milwaukee County officials decided that the old zoo should be replaced, most of the people of Milwaukee agreed. Public money was voted to buy land and build a brand new zoo. The Zoological Society of Milwaukee County, a private organization that had always bought the animals for the Milwaukee Zoo, agreed to provide funds for new animals. Now, as planning and construction of the new zoo began, the Zoo Director had to decide just what kinds of animals should be in it.

Mr. Speidel was sure of one thing—the new zoo would have to show animals in breeding groups. Furthermore, George Speidel wanted the new zoo to specialize in breeding animals that were rarely kept or that rarely reproduced in captivity. Milwaukee already held one breeding record, for polar bears. Polar bears adjust well to captive conditions, and most zoos have always kept one or more. But even today the bears do not often breed in zoos, and when they do, the cubs often die. In 1919, a polar bear cub born in Milwaukee became the first captive-born member of its species to survive to adulthood. The Milwaukee Zoo continued to have success with breeding and raising these animals, and when the new zoo opened, every polar bear on display would be an animal born in Milwaukee.

The Zoo Director wanted to expand on that tradition so

that someday, every animal in the Milwaukee Zoo would be a happy, healthy, captive-born creature who would breed and raise its own young. With that goal in mind, George Speidel set off on a tour of European zoos to find animals for the beautiful new zoo that was taking shape in Milwaukee.

His first stop was the Whipsnade Zoo in England. There Mr. Speidel saw a young female Indian rhinoceros, the second member of her species ever born and successfully raised in captivity. Indian rhinos are a vanishing species in the wild, largely because of illegal hunting. Mr. Speidel knew that there were probably fewer than 500 Indian rhinos left in the world. If Milwaukee could breed these rhinos, the new zoo would be helping to save a rare animal from extinction.

The Whipsnade Zoo had its breeding pair of Indian rhinos, so their young daughter was for sale. Milwaukee's Director wanted the animal. The only question was: Could he locate a mate for her? Luckily, the Basel Zoo in Switzerland had a young male rhino, in fact, the very first Indian rhino born and raised in captivity. The Basel Zoo would sell him so that Milwaukee would have a pair. The young rhino from Switzerland was shipped by air to England to get acquainted with his intended mate and to await the long trip across the ocean.

Meanwhile, George Speidel kept busy, visiting zoos, viewing animals, evaluating Milwaukee's needs, checking the ages and conditions of animals available for sale, and occasionally, making purchases. Finally, after several weeks, he arrived in Hanover, Germany. His trip was almost over. It had been very successful, and Mr. Speidel felt no urgency to make further purchases. It would be pleasant, he thought, to visit the Hanover Zoo as an ordinary zoo-goer, and simply watch the animals.

Then he came to the Primate House. In a large corner cage, a creature with long, lustrous black fur sat with its back to the public. SIAMANG GIBBON (*Hylobates syndactylus*) read the sign next to the cage. (The name *Hylobates*, which means "wood-walker," refers to the genus of gibbons. *Syndactylus,* the species name that identifies siamangs, refers to the webbing between siamangs' toes.) Mr. Speidel wanted a better look at the animal. He cleared his throat, cupped his hands around his mouth, and let out the best possible human imitation of a siamang whoop.

The animal turned its head, then brachiated quickly over to the front of the cage and hung there, staring intently at the strange caller. George Speidel had come face-to-face with Unk.

At once the Zoo Director knew he wanted this siamang for Milwaukee. Was Unk available? The Hanover Zoo was willing to sell him. Although Unk was a popular attraction, all attempts to find him a mate had failed. Nowhere in Europe, it seemed, was there a young female siamang. The Hanover Zoo wanted to use Unk's cage to house a breeding pair of primates.

Now Mr. Speidel had a real dilemma. He wanted Unk for Milwaukee. But he had made himself a promise not to buy animals that would spend their lives in unnatural solitude. He thought about the poor record zoos had with siamangs: Countless animals died before reaching maturity. Others barely existed, sick, unhappy, and alone. The number of recorded births of siamangs in zoos was pitifully small; never had a baby survived more than a few days. He thought about the survival problems wild siamangs faced. Their forest homes in Malaya and Sumatra were being destroyed in response to the needs of growing human populations. The possibility that siamangs would soon be extinct in the wild seemed very real.

Then he looked at Unk. And the decision was made. Mr. Speidel would buy the siamang. Somehow, somewhere, the Milwaukee Zoo would find a mate for Unk.

Unk was to be flown to England and then sent by ship, along with the two Indian rhinos, to the United States. Unk, however, expressed strong disapproval of the plan. He was obviously comfortable and happy in the cage that had been his home for several years and saw no point in exchanging it for a small travel cage. Although Unk weighed only one-third as much as one of his handlers, the seven-year-old siamang was very strong. Besides, he was far more agile than the zookeepers, and had bigger, sharper teeth. He behaved so aggressively when he was being loaded into his shipping cage that Mr. Speidel began to wonder if he had made a mistake. Perhaps Unk had lived alone for too long. Perhaps he was too aggressive ever to live with another siamang.

Eventually, however, the plan was carried out. Unk was flown to England. There he was given a few days to recover from his ordeal before starting a much longer journey. During that time, the siamang recovered the behavior that, with him, passed for good manners.

When the time came for the ocean voyage, the two Indian rhinos walked docilely into their shipping cages. Like many captive rhinos, they were quite tame and not easily upset. Unk's behavior was predictable. He gave the handlers more trouble than the two huge rhinos together. Nevertheless, the young siamang was finally placed in his cage and loaded onto the ship. For the second time in his life, Unk was about to visit the United States, this time to become a permanent resident.

The ship sailed from England on a clear, bright summer day. The weather soon changed. For days on end, the ship pitched and rolled ceaselessly in the heavy seas of a North Atlantic summer storm. It was not the sort of weather designed to bring out the best in Unk's personality. But instead of jumping around, screaming and biting, as everyone had expected, Unk acted frightened and withdrawn. He did not feel well. Like the two rhinos traveling with him, the siamang was seasick.

Bad weather persisted nearly all the way across the Atlantic. Unfortunately for Unk, the journey by water was not

over when the ship reached America. It sailed the St. Law-
rence Seaway to the Great Lakes all the way to Milwaukee.

The animals arrived at the zoo on July 20, 1959. Newspaper and television reporters turned out to see the unload-
ing of the enormous crates that held the rhinos. Much fuss
was made over the arrival of two of the rare creatures. The
difficulties of shipping such large animals over thousands of
miles was enough to make news. The hope that the rhinos
would breed made an even better news story. With all the
excitement over the rhino pair, it was easy for the public
to ignore one seven-year-old siamang gibbon. Unk's arrival
went unheralded except by members of the zoo staff.

In the summer of 1959, most of the new Milwaukee Zoo
was still under construction. The Primate House, however,
was open for business, with a variety of monkeys and apes
in modern enclosures. The new primate cages were spacious
and well-equipped, with shelves, ladders, exercise wheels,
bars, ropes, hanging chains, and tires, giving the intelligent,
active primates many opportunities to play. Each compart-
ment had special controls for light, temperature, and humid-
ity, so that conditions could be properly adjusted for each
species. There were no bars on the cage fronts. Instead there
was thick glass, allowing apes and human visitors to watch
each other freely. The glass served another purpose, too—it
protected the zoo primates from human germs, an important
consideration because many tropical primates are very susceptible to respiratory infections.

Unk was examined by a veterinarian, who pronounced him healthy, if a little difficult to handle. The young siamang was fully recovered from his seasickness, and he quickly settled down in his new enclosure in the Primate House. But most of the people who came to the zoo spent little time watching Unk. They preferred exhibits of monkey families, where there were often babies to watch. Or else they liked Samson, a gorilla who had been in Milwaukee since he was a baby. Now, at age ten, he was a huge, impressive animal. Everyone wanted to watch Samson, the king of the Milwaukee Zoo. Zoo visitors, like the reporters who had greeted Unk, just did not seem very interested in a solitary siamang.

One person who was interested was George Speidel. The Zoo Director had not forgotten his promise to find a mate for Unk. In addition to all his other duties, Mr. Speidel was kept busy corresponding with zoos and animal dealers all over the United States. "We have a beautiful, seven-year-old male siamang gibbon," he wrote. "Do you have a healthy female siamang under the age of ten? If so, we would like to buy her as a mate for Unk, our male."

"Sorry," read dozens of replies. "We have never had much success keeping siamangs. They seem to be too delicate and sensitive to survive in captivity. Our last siamang died after only nine weeks. . . ."

For a while, it looked as if Mr. Speidel would have to give up his dream of breeding siamangs. He would have to be content with the knowledge that the Milwaukee Zoo had one of the few healthy siamangs in captivity anywhere in the world and that Unk seemed reasonably happy in the Primate House. But then, at last, a letter arrived from an animal collector in Seattle, Washington. "I have a six-year-old female siamang," it read. "Suzy is a beautiful, healthy, gentle animal. I would like nothing better than to find her a mate, so I am willing to sell her to the Milwaukee Zoo. However, I have little hope that Suzy will ever become a mother. She has been raised by humans since she was an infant, and now she thinks she is human too. I doubt that she will even recognize another siamang as her own kind. . . ."

George Speidel, of course, had similar worries. But he was pleased to have finally located a suitable female gibbon, and so the deal was made. On March 31, 1960, Suzy arrived by plane from Seattle.

Suzy was a lovely animal. More delicately built than the male Unk, she was nevertheless well-muscled and strong. Her shining dark eyes gave her a gentle, intelligent look, and the conformation of her mouth gave her a permanently wistful expression. She proved to be in excellent health, as promised.

The Milwaukee Zoo staff quickly learned that Suzy's personality was as pleasant as her looks. Although she could be playful, she was relatively quiet and even-tempered, never given to the aggressive outbursts that characterized Unk. All her actions—eating, drinking, grooming herself or her keepers—seemed dainty and calm. Above all, Suzy was incredibly affectionate with humans. She loved to be held or groomed by her keepers and would greet them with kisses.

Unfortunately, Suzy's lovable nature was bound to cause difficulties. She apparently considered herself a human. It might require heroic efforts to convince her that she, like Unk, was a siamang. As a first step, Suzy was placed in a cage next door to Unk. The siamangs could see, but not touch, each other through a glass panel. It was hoped that Unk and Suzy would grow interested in one another and would shortly indicate a desire to live in the same enclosure.

Suzy and Unk seemed perfectly happy with their living arrangements. Each siamang went about its business as it always had. Each related in its own way to the zookeepers. The siamangs ignored each other completely. In those first few days, George Speidel spent many hours watching them. Finally, he thought, he had the two siamangs he wanted. Sadly, he wondered if he would ever have one siamang pair.

CHAPTER FOUR

Mark

It soon became apparent to the zookeepers in the Primate House that the siamang matchmaking plan was not working. Suzy and Unk would not cooperate; in fact, they rarely looked at one another. They obviously needed more encouragement. George Speidel decided to place the two gibbons together in the same cage.

Suzy's enclosure was chosen as the meeting place. Unk regarded his own cage as his territory and could be expected to defend it against any stranger, even an unmated female of his own species. Mr. Speidel hoped Unk would be less aggressive in an unfamiliar place.

One more precaution was taken against Unk's bad temper. Before the meeting, the male siamang was given an injection of a tranquilizer. The dosage of the drug was small: It is always dangerous to medicate a wild animal because there is very little information available on how much will do the job and how much will cause harm. A small dose would minimize the risks to Unk's health. Besides, Mr. Speidel wanted Unk to remain alert, if somewhat calmer than usual.

The keepers held their breath as the door between the two siamang cages was opened. At once, Unk rushed through the doorway. Suzy looked up with interest. Then suddenly her expression turned fearful. Unk was making an "aggressive face" at her—lips drawn back in a frightening grin that revealed his enormous canine teeth.

Suzy scrambled up a rope to a shelf in the middle of her cage. Unk followed and attacked, biting and grabbing. Squealing with fear and confusion, Suzy broke away. But Unk chased after her and attacked again.

Clearly, matters were not proceeding as planned. Unk's tranquilizer had not worked at all—the small, safe dosage had been far too small. Suzy, smaller than Unk, and naturally gentle, could not and would not defend herself. The two animals would have to be separated quickly, before Unk really hurt Suzy. Just as the decision was being made to

separate them, Suzy managed to free herself from Unk's grasp again. This time she headed for the opening between the cages. She tore through the doorway, and before Unk could follow, a keeper pulled a lever dropping the door.

The first meeting between the siamangs was over, and it had been a disaster. Luckily, Suzy proved to be uninjured, if a bit scared. Unk was unmoved by the experience. A few of the zookeepers felt discouraged. George Speidel was discouraged too, but he refused to give up. He decided to wait one month and try to introduce the siamangs again.

For the occasion of the second meeting, Unk received another injection. This time the dosage of tranquilizer was increased. The watching humans waited twenty minutes for the drug to take effect. It seemed to be working: Unk sat quietly in his cage and appeared relaxed and calm.

Mr. Speidel gave the signal to open the cage door. Within seconds Unk was in the doorway, making his aggressive face at Suzy. The encounter was a precise duplicate of the earlier meeting: Unk attacked and Suzy tried frantically to get away. This time, however, the big male gibbon gave her no chance to escape. After what seemed like a very long two minutes, everyone realized that nothing would be accomplished by leaving the animals together. In fact, it seemed essential to separate them quickly to prevent serious or fatal injury to Suzy.

The keeper had no intention of separating the gibbons with his bare hands. Although he outweighed Unk by a hundred pounds, Unk's incredible strength was well-known, and any sensible human regarded the siamang's teeth with respect. Tangling with an enraged Unk would have been foolhardy in the extreme.

Nevertheless, the keeper had to get Unk away from Suzy, and fast. He picked up a hose and turned on the water, directing a strong stream right at Unk through an opening at the bottom of the cage. Siamangs, like other apes, do not enjoy getting wet, and Unk was no exception. Immediately he forgot all about mauling Suzy. With no other objective than escaping the hateful spray, he dashed back into his own cage.

Meeting Number Two had proved as disastrous as the first. Most of the zoo staff despaired of ever getting the siamangs together. They could not continue to increase Unk's tranquilizer dosage. Too much would make him sleep, and when he woke up, he was certain to be as bad-tempered as ever. Besides, only good luck had prevented injury to Suzy during the first two encounters. Sooner or later Unk was certain to hurt her. Nearly all the humans involved in the project wanted to give up.

George Speidel had to admit that the situation looked hopeless. Perhaps he should listen to advice and forget the idea of a pair of siamangs. He thought about the problem for weeks. But no solution came. Then one day he told the siamangs' story to a friend, who suggested a completely new way of viewing Unk's behavior.

Adult male siamang gibbons are normally bad-tempered toward unfamiliar animals. They have to be aggressive if they are to be successful defenders of a family territory in the jungle. In the wild, very docile male siamangs are probably not successful breeders. Unk, however, was far more aggressive than normal. After all, a wild male siamang without a mate should not attack an unmated female. If that were normal behavior, new siamang pairs would not be formed and the species would quickly die out.

Why was Unk's behavior abnormal? Was it because he had been raised by humans, without a chance to learn normal siamang behavior? Perhaps he just did not know when aggression was appropriate and when it was not.

However, there was another possible explanation for Unk's behavior. Perhaps his body produced male hormones in unusually large quantity. Hormones are substances produced in special glands in the bodies of animals (including humans). Some hormones are important in controlling physical processes such as growth and digestion. Some appear to affect behavior.

Most hormones are produced by animals of both sexes, but a few are produced only by females, a few only by males. Sex hormones help to create specific physical characteristics, but in animals whose behavior is largely controlled by hormones, sex hormones help to produce appropriate behavior as well. The ability of a female bird to lay eggs, for example, depends on female hormones, but so might her method of building a nest. Similarly, the physical ability of a male bird to fertilize eggs depends on male hormones, but so might his singing. In siamangs, aggression might well be dependent on the body's production of male hormones. Too much aggression, as in Unk's case, could mean that the body was overproducing male hormones.

The actions of hormones on animals' bodies, and especially on animals' behavior, are not very well understood, but biology researchers agree that male and female hormones often appear to counteract one another. Therefore, an animal's overproduction of male hormones might be treated by giving him injections of female hormones. (No one has figured out how to make an animal's body reduce its production of male hormones.)

Mr. Speidel decided to try female hormone treatment for Unk. The siamang would receive only a small amount of female hormones, not enough to produce female behavior or physical characteristics, just enough to reduce his aggressive behavior to the point where he would not attack Suzy when they met. Mr. Speidel knew that not only could hormone treatments have an effect on an animal's behavior, but also that a change in the animal's social situation could have a permanent effect on hormone levels. In other words, hormones affect behavior, but behavior affects hormones as well. If, after hormone treatment, Unk formed a pair bond with Suzy, his normal siamang behavior in a normal gibbon social arrangement might reduce his body's overproduction of male hormones.

For three days, Unk received daily treatments of female hormone. The following day he was given an injection of a stronger tranquilizer than he had received before. Suzy also received a small dose of tranquilizer in case memories of the two attacks made her nervous.

Unk's tranquilizer quickly took effect. The siamang slumped to the floor of his cage, half asleep. He was too groggy to protest as he was moved into Suzy's enclosure. Suzy watched him warily, eyes wide, but made no move to approach him.

After a while Unk began to stir. The effects of the tranquilizer were wearing off. Still sleepy and wobbly, Unk stood up. To the human observers, he looked as if he were about to attack once again. He must have looked that way to Suzy also, because all at once, she took matters into her own hands. Before the groggy Unk could reach her, she charged at him and bit him hard on the foot.

Gentle Suzy had finally had enough. The zookeepers were amazed and pleased. And apparently Unk was, too. From that moment on, he made no attempt to attack. He accepted Suzy's companionship and she accepted his. The introduction had been successful at last. The Milwaukee Zoo had a siamang pair. The question now became: Would this pair, raised by humans, understand enough about normal siamang behavior to breed and raise their young?

By the time a week had gone by, it was hard for the zoo-keepers to remember why they had felt pessimistic about the siamangs. Unk and Suzy were truly a pair, and, typical of gibbon pairs, they seemed absolutely devoted to one another, head over heels in love.

The siamangs played together, chasing each other all over their enclosure, and wrestling, squealing all the while. Zoo visitors, watching them, sometimes thought that Unk and Suzy were fighting. In some ways, the siamangs' play did resemble Unk's terrible attacks on Suzy, but close observation revealed an important difference. Unk's expression was not his aggressive face, but rather his play face. To make the play face, he drew back the corners of his lips in a kind of grin, but he did not open his mouth so wide as he did for the aggressive face. His imposing teeth did not show as much as they did when he threatened.

During quiet times, Suzy and Unk often touched one another. They spent hours grooming together. They slept together on a shelf, hugging each other close. They embraced frequently, wrapping their long arms around one another. The siamangs loved the sun, and a favorite sitting place was a patch of cage floor where the sun's rays entered through a roof skylight. When Suzy sat in the sunlight, Unk often sat down beside her and put his arm around her shoulders.

Just like a wild pair of gibbons, Unk and Suzy had a territory to defend. Of course, their territory was man-made and there was no possibility of losing it to another siamang

family. Neither of these facts seemed to matter at all to Suzy and Unk. They were as happy in their enclosure as any pair in the jungle, and every morning and evening they proclaimed their proud ownership of their home.

The siamangs' calling sessions often lasted half an hour or more. Both animals seemed to enjoy themselves immensely as they swung and jumped about the cage creating a racket. Humans who listened carefully quickly realized that the siamang choruses were not merely random noise. Instead, they were songs with definite patterns of sounds marking beginning, middle, and end. Also, there were different parts for male and female voices. Suzy's calling consisted mainly of a rhythmic series of barks which she varied from time to time by moving her hands in front of her mouth to change the tones. Unk's calling built to a crescendo of ear-splitting noises that sounded like *ya-hoo.*

All this evidence of normal siamang pair behavior made George Speidel very happy. At last there was good reason to believe that his plan could work. Everything was going well, so perhaps it was just a matter of time before Unk and Suzy became parents.

A calm and uneventful year passed for the siamangs at the Milwaukee Zoo. Both animals seemed happy and healthy. They got along perfectly with one another. Suzy continued to be friendly and gentle with humans, although now that she had a gibbon mate, she was somewhat less affectionate with people. Having a mate apparently agreed with Unk.

His relationship with the zookeepers improved enormously. While it was still a good idea to be careful around the strong, unpredictable ape, the keepers noticed that Unk wore his play face far more often than his aggressive face.

In the fall of 1961, when Suzy was about seven-and-a-half years old, and probably reaching physical maturity, the siamangs mated for the first time. By winter, the primate keepers began to suspect that Suzy was pregnant. The veterinarian who examined her confirmed that she was.

The available information on siamang pregnancies and births was minimal. No one knew how long the normal gestation period was for siamangs, so no one could predict with certainty just when Suzy's baby would be born. Knowing that the normal gestation period of larger apes was around eight months or a little more, and the gestation period of smaller gibbons around seven months, Mr. Speidel reasoned that a siamang's pregnancy might last around seven-and-a-half months. Suzy's baby would most likely be born in early summer.

Meanwhile, there was nothing to do but wait and read as much information as possible about the care of newborn apes. Mr. Speidel realized that there was some chance Suzy would reject her baby. Nearly all the gorillas and many of the chimpanzees born in captivity up to that time had been raised by humans. The little apes' mothers had grown up in zoos, isolated from the social groups in which normal ape behavior is learned. They had simply never learned how to care for their young.

Suzy had spent most of her life with humans. She had had no opportunity to observe her own mother taking care of younger sisters and brothers. It was quite possible that she would show no interest in her baby.

Unk was a further complication. Chimpanzee and gorilla fathers play no role in raising their children, but gibbon fathers do. Unk too had grown up outside a normal siamang family, and had had no chance to learn how to be a father. It was possible that he would try to harm the baby. So, even if Suzy proved to be a good mother, the baby might have to be taken from her.

On July 10, 1962, after a gestation period of 230 days (seven-and-a-half months), the baby was born. Suzy gave birth on a shelf along the back wall of the enclosure, picking a safe and secluded spot high in the air, as a siamang mother would do in the jungle. She behaved calmly and expertly, as if she had witnessed a hundred births. Unk watched protectively, making no attempt to interfere.

The newborn baby was unbelievably tiny—the primate keepers estimated its weight at six ounces, less than half a pound. It had almost no hair, just a patch of black fuzz on the top of its head. The keepers could not help but think that this was a pretty pathetic-looking little creature. Nevertheless, the newborn siamang was alert and bright-eyed, and appeared to be in good health. No humans were permitted inside the cage for fear of upsetting Unk and Suzy. Everyone wanted to encourage the siamangs to take care of their child, and the best way of doing that was to leave them alone for a few weeks.

Suzy proved to be an excellent mother, caring for her tiny infant calmly, and with great gentleness. She seemed confident and happy as she nursed the baby, groomed and cuddled it. In its first few weeks of life, the baby was too small and weak to leave Suzy, so there was little for Unk to do in his new role as a father. Still, he behaved protectively toward his family and seemed interested in the baby. Any fears that Unk would be jealous of the infant or try to harm it proved unfounded.

Naturally, the members of the zoo staff were very excited about the siamang baby. And so were the people of Milwaukee. At last, the press had a ready-made news story about the siamangs. Reporters wanted all the facts about the infant. Was it a boy or a girl? What was its name?

Not wanting to disturb the siamang family, the zookeepers had not been able to examine the baby. They couldn't tell if it was male or female, and so they thought it best to wait until it was older to name it. And of course it didn't matter to Suzy and Unk if their child had a human name. But it did matter to the public. So the keepers decided to name the baby Mark.

Little Mark developed rapidly. Within a few weeks the baby's hair grew in thick and black (although a siamang's long adult hair does not appear until the animal is two or

three years old). Mark began to venture away from Suzy for short periods of time, tentatively exploring the environment.

Now that the baby was older, Unk began to take a more active role in family life. He sometimes played with Mark, but very gently, seeming to realize that the small animal could not endure rough treatment. He was remarkably tolerant of the baby, allowing Mark to hang on his fur or climb over his face without punishment.

Within months, zoo officials were certain that Suzy and Unk were good parents. Mark was obviously healthy and well-nourished, and seemed normal in every way. However, as the baby began to move about the enclosure, the zookeepers made an interesting discovery: Mark was most definitely a girl. Should she be re-named? The public knew the baby as Mark. On the other hand, Mark was a strange name for a female animal.

In the end, it was decided to let the name remain. After all, the baby was the very first siamang born and raised by its mother in captivity. She had truly made a *mark* on the zoo world.

The zoo world agreed. Every year, the American Association of Zoological Parks and Aquariums gives an award to a zoo that breeds a rare animal. In 1962, two AAZPA awards were given. One went to the Portland, Oregon Zoo for the birth of an Indian elephant. The other award went to the Milwaukee Zoo for the birth of a siamang gibbon named Mark.

CHAPTER FIVE

A Growing Family

Mark was a happy, playful baby, probably very much like wild siamang babies in Sumatra. Under the watchful eye of her mother, she climbed all around the zoo enclosure, but always returned to Suzy after a few minutes for reassurance. Like all little apes, Mark seemed to need a lot of physical contact with her mother—hugging, patting, nursing, grooming. Zoo officials felt very relieved that the siamangs' family life was so normal. They knew too well the psychological problems young apes can develop when they are rejected by their mothers.

61

By the time Mark was three months old, she had begun to sample adult siamang food—apples, oranges, bananas, onions, sweet potatoes, lettuce, bread, and sunflower seeds. In the wild, small gibbon species like white-handed gibbons eat more fruit than leaves. Siamangs eat more leaves and greenery. But in the zoo, siamangs and white-handed gibbons receive essentially identical diets, and both species seem to thrive. Some zoo siamangs like greens such as lettuce best, while others prefer fruits they would never see in their native habitat, such as oranges or apples. Each ape has its own favorite foods. Little Mark liked bananas.

Of course, bananas were not yet an important part of her diet. She was still an infant and, although she was developing perhaps three times as fast as a human infant, her main source of nourishment remained her mother's milk. Gradually, over a period of months, Mark began to eat more adult food. By the time she was a year old she was not dependent on Suzy's milk. She would continue to nurse for comfort as long as Suzy would allow it, probably until the next baby was born. But for all practical purposes, Mark was weaned.

Throughout Mark's infancy, the siamang family was left alone. The animals were not handled by the zookeepers. Except for feeding the gibbons and cleaning their enclosure, humans did not enter the family's territory. Everyone wanted conditions at the zoo to be as close as possible to conditions in the jungle. The benefits of this policy were apparent: Unk and Suzy and their daughter behaved very much like wild gibbons.

When Mark was just about one year old, Unk and Suzy mated again. On March 20, 1964, their second baby was born. Again the siamangs were model parents, and zoo officials saw no reason to interfere with the family. The adult animals had been successful in raising Mark; they could certainly handle a second child. Everyone looked forward to watching the two young siamangs growing up together.

Eighteen days later the new baby died. The zookeepers realized the baby was dead before Suzy did. She clutched it tightly, struggling to hold it when the keepers took it away. A *post mortem* examination revealed that the baby had died of pneumonia, a very common cause of death among apes.

Even in the wild, pneumonia probably kills many newborn gibbons. Tiny, hairless babies are very susceptible to chills as their mothers swing through damp treetops. A high rate of infant mortality keeps the siamang population from growing too large for the available territory.

Of course, there was no danger of siamang overpopulation in the zoo. Everyone would have been happy to make space for more siamangs, so the baby's death was a sad and disappointing event. Fortunately, Suzy quickly recovered from her distress over the loss of her baby, and within a few months was pregnant again. The new baby was born on Christmas Day, but within five days, it too died of pneumonia.

Suzy's fourth pregnancy resulted in the birth of a baby on May 31, 1966. The infant was considerably smaller than it should have been, and its eyes were shut tight. It was estimated that the little gibbon had been born one month prematurely. The chances for its survival were slim, and before zoo officials had time to decide if there was some way to help it, the baby died. It had lived only a few hours.

George Speidel began to think that perhaps Mark's survival and good health had been a lucky accident. He wondered if she was the only child Unk and Suzy would ever raise. On May 22, 1967, yet another infant was born. Unlike the premature baby, this one seemed perfectly healthy and normal. Still, the two that died of pneumonia had been healthy at birth also.

A few people thought that the new baby should be removed from the siamang family and cared for by humans. This might have prevented death from pneumonia, but Mr. Speidel thought that the baby belonged with its family. Suzy was able to take care of an infant siamang better than any human foster mother.

A week passed. The baby seemed fine. A second week went by and the little siamang remained healthy. After three weeks with no problems, Mr. Speidel was sure the baby would live. Reporters were invited to see the new siamang, and a picture of the infant was printed on the front page of a Milwaukee newspaper. The baby was not named immediately because no one wanted to make the same mistake they had made in naming Mark. But after a few more weeks, when it was determined that the baby was a male, he was named Smitty, in honor of the photographer who snapped the front-page picture.

Mark was almost five years old when Smitty was born, and the interest she showed in the new baby seemed as much motherly as sisterly. Her little brother appeared to fascinate her. She constantly tried to touch him and hold him.

At first, Suzy barely permitted her daughter to look at the baby. Smitty was too small to play and needed his mother's attention at all times. Suzy pushed Mark away whenever she reached out to touch the baby.

It must have been a frustrating time for Mark. Luckily, though, she was a member of a family, and her need for contact with other siamangs was met partly by Unk, her father. During the first few weeks after Smitty's birth, Unk and Mark spent a great deal of time together.

Smitty grew quickly. Within a few months he became the most active, playful little ape the zookeepers had ever seen. Although Suzy still watched him carefully, she readily allowed Mark to hold and groom him. As far as Smitty was concerned, however, sitting quietly in his sister's lap was not nearly as rewarding as active play. He seemed to enjoy squirming out of Mark's determined grasp and then teasing his sister until she chased him wildly all over the enclosure.

On September 13, 1969, when Mark was seven years old and Smitty was two, another siamang baby was born. The

baby proved to be a male, and was named Les, after the supervisor of the Primate House.

Shortly after Les was born, the Milwaukee siamangs became the subjects of a scientific study. Greysolynne Fox was a graduate student at a university in Milwaukee. She wanted to become a primate ethologist, a scientist who investigates and compares the behavior of different species of monkeys and apes.

The Milwaukee siamangs were perfect subjects for her zoo study. Information on wild siamangs was practically nonexistent. But as far as anyone could tell, the Milwaukee animals were much like their wild counterparts. Scientists had already collected a large amount of data on wild white-handed gibbons. By observing the Milwaukee siamangs, Greysolynne Fox could accomplish several goals: She could collect data on the behavior of siamangs; compare siamang and white-handed gibbon behavior; and gain valuable experience in watching siamangs. She hoped she would soon have a chance to study wild siamangs. Then she would be able to compare not only wild siamangs with wild white-handed gibbons, but also wild siamangs with captive siamangs.

The first discovery Greysolynne made was that the siamangs were extraordinarily interested in her. If she stood directly in front of the enclosure to get a good view of the animals, the siamangs immediately stopped whatever they were doing and came over to investigate her. They stood close to the glass and peered out intently. They put their hands on the window, apparently trying to touch her. Sometimes they licked the glass. Mark and Smitty performed for her, running off to brachiate around the cage and turn somersaults, then running back to the front of the enclosure to make sure she was watching. When Greysolynne placed her notebook on a ledge in front of the cage glass, the siamangs watched in fascination as she wrote. When she set a furry hat on the ledge, the siamangs tried to groom it through the glass.

The first time Greysolynne tried to tape record the siamangs' calling sessions, she set up her machine next to the shift cage, a small, barred cage connecting the two large enclosures. (A shift cage is used as a passageway when keepers want to move animals from one enclosure to another without handling them.) At once, Unk and Suzy came over to investigate, reaching out underneath the bars and trying to push the buttons on the tape recorder. Unk also revealed a fondness for rude pinching.

The purpose of the investigation was to learn about the siamangs' interactions with one another, not with humans, so Greysolynne made some adjustments. She learned to stand off to one side of the enclosure and speak her notes into a tape recorder instead of writing them. When she recorded the siamangs' voices, she made sure to place the tape recorder (and herself) out of the gibbons' reach. When she wanted to photograph the animals, she asked the photographer to set up his cameras half an hour early so that the siamangs had a chance to complete their through-the-glass inspection of the equipment and return to their normal behavior.

Sometimes, when Greysolynne Fox stood recording her observations about the siamangs, zoo visitors would stop to ask what she was doing. "How can you tell the animals apart?" was a common question. "They all look alike to me." Greysolynne would explain how she had very quickly learned to tell which siamang was which by head shape, amount of hair on head and body and patterns of hair distribution, and skin coloring on the face. It seemed to her that siamang looks were as individual as human looks. Of course, after a while, the siamangs could also be distinguished by their personalities. Each animal had its favorite spots in the enclosure, favorite foods, favorite pastimes. Suzy, for example, was quieter and played less than either Unk or the children. However, she loved to twirl around on a rope that hung from the top of the cage. When the rope was removed because it posed a danger to the young animals, Suzy began to hang by one hand from the overhead bars and twirl around on her own arm.

Because Les was a newborn baby when the study began, it was possible for Greysolynne Fox to keep detailed records on infant siamang development and on changing relationships within the ape family. Until Les was nearly three months old, Greysolynne never saw him leave Suzy's body. When he was not nursing or sleeping, he sometimes sucked his thumb or his big toe. During this time, Unk appeared to be totally uninterested in the baby. Perhaps experience with earlier offspring had taught him not to expect much response from such a young infant.

Les' older brother and sister, however, displayed none of Unk's indifference. Smitty, who had never seen an infant before, was fascinated. He inspected Les with his eyes, nose, and hands while the baby clung to Suzy. Mark too reached out for the baby, but she was not permitted to touch him. Often, Suzy bit her daughter to chase her away from Les.

In December, when he was three months old and had several teeth, Les sampled his first solid food. He also began to leave his mother for short periods of time, although Suzy watched him constantly. He became more of a playmate for his brother. Smitty appeared to enjoy tugging the baby to his feet by an arm or a leg. And at last, Mark was permitted to hold the baby. Sometimes, Suzy allowed her daughter to take care of Les for an hour or more, while she took a twirling break, or groomed Unk, or ate a leisurely meal.

Regardless of her usefulness as a baby sitter, Mark was no longer a real part of the family. It was obvious that she was being pushed out. Because siamangs enjoy being groomed, Mark was allowed to groom the others as much as she wanted. However, none of the other animals would groom her in return. When she approached another siamang, asking to be groomed, she was either ignored or attacked. At feeding time, she was not permitted to eat with the group. Usually Unk, Suzy holding the baby, and Smitty would eat

together near the front of the cage. Mark sat far away, at the back of the enclosure or on a raised platform. If she tried to join the group, Unk threatened her with his aggressive face. If she persisted, she might be bitten. Suzy and Smitty also chased Mark away. The keepers had to be sure to toss food to different parts of the enclosure so Mark got enough to eat.

When Mark held Les, the rest of the siamangs were slightly more tolerant, allowing her to rejoin the group briefly. Sometimes, when the animals were not feeding, Smitty played with his sister. But most of the time Mark was isolated.

In contrast, Smitty was an important part of the family group. His high spirits and juvenile bad manners were accepted without protest from his parents. At feeding time, he was permitted to take food away from Unk, Suzy, and even the baby. His need for physical contact was indulged; while he ate, he kept a hand on Unk or Suzy.

All this was normal behavior for a siamang family. Nevertheless, it was hard on Mark. In the wild, she could have left her family group, but in the zoo there was no place for her to go. And zoo officials did not want to remove her to a cage by herself, because she needed company.

Over the next few months, Les developed from a helpless infant into an adventurous child. Greysolynne Fox noticed that he was always experimenting, finding out just what marvelous feats a gibbon body could accomplish. But for quite some time, he always made sure to hang onto some support with at least three limbs. Only when he was eight months old did he begin to brachiate in grown-up fashion, using only two hands. Les also learned to assert himself in games with his older brother. When Smitty tugged too roughly on the baby's leg, Les threatened by exposing his canine teeth in his own version of the aggressive face.

Les' relationship with his sister was calmer. He seemed to enjoy spending time with Mark. For her part, Mark treated the baby gently and affectionately. It was fortunate for her that Les liked her company, for only when the two were together did the hostility of the parent animals subside. In general, however, Unk behaved aggressively toward his daughter more often with each passing day.

In June 1971, a new baby was born. It lived only three days, dying of pneumonia. Unk and Suzy mated again almost immediately. Major changes would soon take place in the siamang family.

During the fall, Mark was placed under increasing stress. Suzy acted hostile toward her, and Mark learned to avoid her mother. Unk's hostility was harder to avoid. Her father began to kick her, hanging from a bar by his hands and swinging his feet into her chest. He sometimes chased her around the enclosure, forcing her to retreat into the shift cage. Three times, he even followed her into the shift cage and continued to attack.

Les spent more and more time with his sister. It seemed to Greysolynne Fox that the little siamang sought Mark's company most when Unk acted especially violent toward her. Perhaps Les was trying to make her feel better.

When a new baby was born on February 5, 1972, Suzy and the infant were separated from the family. Zoo officials thought that the playful activities of Smitty and Les combined with Unk's aggressiveness toward Mark might be more excitement than a newborn ape could tolerate. So, Suzy and the baby were placed in the secondary siamang enclosure. They could enter the shift cage, but a wire mesh separated them from the rest of the family.

Suzy began to spend all her time in the shift cage, pressed up against the barrier that separated her from Unk. Unk missed her, too. He sat on the ledge next to the shift cage entrance, and the two siamangs pushed their fingers through the holes in the mesh to touch one another. Suzy and Unk sat for hours holding hands this way. Unk was so concerned over his separation from Suzy that he ignored Mark completely. Suzy also seemed more concerned over her separation from Unk than anything else, including her infant. She did not hurt the baby, but she handled it less carefully than she had her other children.

Nevertheless, the baby was healthy. It was a male, and he was named Sam, for a primate keeper who loved the siamangs most of all his charges. In a few months, Suzy and little Sam rejoined the rest of the family.

Mark was undoubtedly interested in the baby, just as she had been when Les and Smitty were very small. But she also understood what to expect if she approached her mother, so she stayed clear of Suzy and Sam. Smitty was not so cautious. He wanted to see the baby and approached Suzy directly. However, when he came too close to the newborn, a strange thing happened—Unk attacked, but he attacked Mark, not Smitty.

Unk's violence toward his daughter had resumed, stronger than ever. Zoo officials realized that Mark's safety was in question. Three days after Suzy and Sam were returned to the family, Mark was removed and placed by herself in the adjoining enclosure.

Suzy continued to behave rather casually toward Sam. Instead of keeping him clutched to her chest, she often carried him around on her leg. Poor little Sam held on as well as he could, his fingers wrapped around the hair on Suzy's thigh. Sometimes, Suzy sat with Sam on her foot, tapping the foot on the floor. The baby bounced around and occasionally fell off. Perhaps Suzy was getting old and one last baby had tried her patience. Still, she must have cared for him well enough, because he developed as quickly as Mark, Smitty, and Les.

As little Sam was developing from an infant into a juvenile siamang, Smitty was becoming an adult. He became less playful and slightly more dignified. Greysolynne Fox had noticed that the siamangs did not usually play alone and that two animals played together more often than three. When Sam was very young, Smitty and Les were the most frequent play partners. Later, Les played with Sam.

Greysolynne especially enjoyed watching Les and Sam foot wrestle. In this game, the two siamangs faced each other as they hung by their hands from the top bars of the cage. Then they kicked out, each trying to hit the soles of the other's feet with his own. Sometimes they used their wonderfully agile, grasping feet to grab at an opponent's ankle. When Les and Sam swung back and forth as they foot wrestled, it reminded Greysolynne of a ballet.

Greysolynne began to look for signs of aggression toward Smitty. He was growing up, and Unk and Suzy could be expected to push him out of the family as they had done with Mark. But although Smitty did not spend as much time with his parents as he once had, the intense hostility that Mark had experienced did not develop. Greysolynne and the zookeepers agreed that Unk and Suzy probably would not have more babies. They were more than twenty years old and beginning to show signs of old age. If the family size were to remain stable, perhaps Smitty's continued presence would not be a threat. (Months later, this theory was proven incorrect, when Unk began displaying hostility toward Smitty. Someday, he too would have to be removed from the family group.)

As for Mark, living alone was not satisfactory. A social animal who had grown up in a family group, she was obviously depressed by herself. Zoo officials began to look around for suitable companionship for her. They soon learned that officials of the Cincinnati Zoo wanted to breed siamangs. They already had one female, and in the fall of 1973, they acquired a five-year-old male named Chiffy from a primate research center.

The Cincinnati Zoo would be glad to take Mark on a permanent breeding loan. This meant she would live in Cincinnati, and if she produced young, half the offspring would stay at the Cincinnati Zoo and half would be sent to Milwaukee. By sending Mark away, the Milwaukee Zoo was not only giving one animal a chance for a happier life, but also helping to insure a growing zoo population of a rare species.

In January 1974, Mark arrived in Cincinnati. At first she was placed in a cage with the other female. Both animals seemed happy to have company and got along well from the start. Chiffy was placed in an adjacent cage, separated from the females by only a wire mesh. When no hostility developed, the three siamangs were placed together.

It was practically a case of love at first sight. Mark and Chiffy formed a pair bond and ignored the other female completely (she finally was removed). Chiffy was still quite young, and probably not fully matured physically, so the zookeepers knew that the siamangs might not reproduce for two or three more years. But Mark and Chiffy behaved like normal gibbon mates. In both Cincinnati and Milwaukee, zoo people could look forward with confidence to a second generation of zoo-born siamangs.

CHAPTER SIX

The Future
for Siamangs

Siamang gibbons are rare animals. In contrast to white-handed gibbons, which are found throughout Southeast Asia, wild siamangs exist in only two places—the Malayan Peninsula and the island of Sumatra.

The Sumatran and Malayan jungle homes of siamangs are shrinking every day, destroyed by human hands. In some places, jungles are cleared to create farmland, desperately needed to provide food for skyrocketing human populations. Some jungles are cleared so people can obtain the valuable lumber from the tall trees. In some places, jungles are destroyed in the search for oil to serve an energy-hungry world.

A jungle is a fragile environment. Once it is destroyed, it is gone forever, or at least permanently altered in important ways. Jungle soil is surprisingly thin, and it is held in place almost entirely by the roots of enormous trees. When the trees are cut, soil is quickly washed away, making jungles very poor farmland. The tall trees do not grow again, so jungle lumbering is hardly a long-term business. And once the oil is gone, there is nothing left but dry wells surrounded by desolation.

A few kinds of wild creatures seem to adjust reasonably well to radically altered environments. White-handed gibbons, for example, seem willing to live very close to farmland. But most wild creatures cannot adapt. Without the jungle, there would be no siamangs, no orangutans, no tigers on Sumatra.

The siamangs' chances for survival in the wild are totally dependent on wildlife preserves—special areas set aside by governments to be left in a natural state, the plants and animals undisturbed by humans. Probably nearly all of the siamangs in the wild today live in or around preserves in Malaya and Sumatra. For now, the siamang gibbons are safe.

But unless the problems of human overpopulation and overconsumption of natural resources are solved soon, the pressures may become too great. Governments may consider wildlife preserves expensive luxuries they can no longer afford. Wildlife preserves, like the rest of the jungles, may be destroyed to buy a few more years of population growth and overconsumption for unthinking humanity. If the preserves should disappear, wild siamang gibbons would soon become extinct.

A principal concern of good zoos today is extinction-prevention. Zoo people do whatever they can to educate the public about wildlife conservation, to encourage governments to maintain wildlife preserves, and most of all to breed rare animals in captivity. If the Milwaukee Zoo has anything to say about it, there will always be room in the world for siamang gibbons.

ALICE SCHICK lives with her husband Joel and numerous animals (predominantly cats) in Monterey, Massachusetts. She is the author of *Kongo and Kumba: Two Gorillas*, *The Peregrine Falcons*, and co-author of *The Remarkable Ride of Israel Bissell as Related by Molly the Crow*.

JOEL SCHICK would rather draw animals than anything else. He is a book designer as well as the illustrator of many books, including *The Gobble-uns'll Git You Ef You Don't Watch Out!*, *The Remarkable Ride of Israel Bissell as Related by Molly the Crow*, and *Derek Koogar Was a Star*.